Edward Dowden, Percy Bysshe Shelley, Thomas James Wise

Review of Hogg's

Edward Dowden, Percy Bysshe Shelley, Thomas James Wise

Review of Hogg's

ISBN/EAN: 9783337167783

Printed in Europe, USA, Canada, Australia, Japan

Cover: Foto ©ninafisch / pixelio.de

More available books at **www.hansebooks.com**

REVIEW OF HOGG'S

'Memoirs of Prince Alexy Haimatoff"

BY

PERCY BYSSHE SHELLEY

TOGETHER WITH AN EXTRACT FROM

"*SOME EARLY WRITINGS OF SHELLEY*"

BY

PROFESSOR E DOWDEN LL.D

Edited

WITH AN INTRODUCTORY NOTE

BY

THOMAS J WISE

London

PUBLISHED FOR THE SHELLEY SOCIETY

BY REEVES AND TURNER 196 STRAND

1886

CONTENTS.

INTRODUCTORY NOTE.

INTRODUCTORY NOTE.

PROFESSOR DOWDEN has stated so fully—both in his original *Contemporary Review* article, and in the *Postscript* which he has now added to our reprint of it—the circumstances which led him to light upon Shelley's Review, and to prove with sufficient accuracy its authorship, that little remains to be recounted here. Suffice it to say briefly, that in 1813 Hogg published pseudonymously a novel,[1] of the title-page of which the following is a transcript :—

> Memoirs / of / Prince Alexy Haimatoff. / Translated from / the original Latin MSS. / under the immediate inspection of / the Prince, / By / John Brown, Esq. / . . . . / London : / Printed for T. Hookham, / 15, Old Bond Street, / 1813.

---

[1] Not the only Romance of which he was the author.

The collation is :—

> 12mo. Title (with imprint on verso—"S.
> Gosnell, Printer, Little Queen Street, Lon-
> don"); Preface pp. iii—iv. ; and pp. 1—236
> of Text.

The imprint is repeated at the foot of the last
page.

This book received an appreciative and somewhat
lengthy notice in *The Critical Review*,[1] vol. vi, No. vi,
December, 1814,—Article vii, pp. 566—574 ; and the
authorship of this review has, as is now well known,
been traced home to Shelley. The Review is here
reprinted verbatim, without alteration or correction
of any kind whatever, save only where a word is
distinctly mis-spelt, in which case the fact of its
correction is noted at the foot of the page. The
punctuation is most erratic, and the errors on that
account are many and grave; but I think that for

---

[1] The / Critical Review : / or, / Annals / of / Literature. / Series
the Fourth. / Vol. vi. / London : / Printed for the Proprietors, / By
Thomas Bluck, 2, Paternoster Row ; / Published by G. & S. Robinson,
Paternoster Row ; / 1814. / (July to December.)   Octavo.   Half-
Title, Title, and pp. 1—700 ; followed by an Index, consisting of
six unnumbered pages.

these the printer and his reader are as likely as Shelley to be accountable. Only upon *one* occsion have I ventured to interfere with the original stops (page 23, line 8) ; and it will be seen that I have there placed within brackets the semi-colon which I have considered it advisable to insert.

Publicly attributed to Shelley only in September, 1884, this most interesting piece of the poet's early prose writing has never yet been incorporated in any edition of his *Works ;* and it is matter for congratulation that the Committee of the Shelley Society have, thus early in the Society's existence, found an opportunity of reproducing a fugitive essay of so much character in a convenient and accessible form.

The *Memoirs of Prince Alexy Haimatoff* itself is an exceedingly scarce volume, and I believe that I am correct in stating that only two copies are at present publicly known to be in existence. Of these, one is in the possession of Hogg's daughter, Mrs. Lonsdale ; and the other is preserved in the British Museum. Though obtained for that institution on November 16th, 1878—as the date stamped

B 2

upon it testifies—it was not until after the publication of Professor Dowden's article that the book was in any way connected with its author's real name.

The essay by Professor Dowden which occupies pp. 31—52 of this brochure, is the second portion of an article which appeared in *The Contemporary Review*, for September, 1884, pp. 383—396 ; and for permission to reprint which upon the present occasion, the Society is indebted to the Professor's courtesy.

THOMAS J. WISE.

127, *Devonshire Road, Holloway, N.*

SHELLEY'S REVIEW OF

"Memoirs of Prince Alexy Haimatoff."

"𝕸𝖊𝖒𝖔𝖎𝖗𝖘 𝖔𝖋 𝕻𝖗𝖎𝖓𝖈𝖊 𝕬𝖑𝖊𝖝𝖞 𝕳𝖆𝖎𝖒𝖆𝖙𝖔𝖋𝖋."

Memoirs of Prince Alexy Haimatoff. Translated
from the original Latin MSS. under the immediate ‿ inspection of the Prince. By JOHN
BROWN, ESQ. Pp. 236. 12mo. Hookham,
1814.

Is the suffrage of mankind the legitimate criterion
of intellectual energy? Are complaints of the aspirants to literary fame, to be considered as the
honourable disappointment of neglected genius, or
the sickly impatience of a dreamer miserably self
deceived? the most illustrious ornaments of the
annals of the human race, have been stigmatised by
the contempt and abhorrence of entire communities
of man; but this injustice arose out of some temporary superstition, some partial interest, some
national doctrine: a glorious redemption awaited

their remembrance. There is indeed, nothing so remarkable in the contempt of the ignorant for the enlightened : the vulgar pride of folly, delights to triumph upon mind. This is an intelligible process : the infancy or ingloriousness that can be thus explained, detracts nothing from the beauty of virtue or the sublimity of genius. But what does utter obscurity express ? if the public do not advert even in censure to a performance, has that performance already received its condemnation ?

The result of this controversy is important to the ingenuous critic. His labours are indeed, miserably worthless, if their objects may invariably be attained before their application. He should know the limits of his prerogative. He should not be ignorant, whether it is his duty to promulgate the decisions of others, or to cultivate his taste and judgment that he may be enabled to render a reason for his own.

Circumstances the least connected with intellectual nature have contributed, for a certain period, to retain in obscurity, the most memorable specimens of human genius. The author re[f]rains perhaps from introducing his production to the world with all the pomp of empirical bibliopolism. A sudden tide in the affairs of men may make the neglect or contradiction of some insignificant doctrine, a badge of obscurity and discredit : those even who are exempt from the action of these absurd predilections, are necessarily in an indirect manner affected by their influence. It is perhaps the product of an imagination daring and undisciplined : the majority of readers ignorant and disdaining toleration refuse to pardon a neglect of common rules ; their canons of criticism are carelessly infringed, it is less religious than a charity sermon, less methodical and cold than a French tragedy, where all the unities are preserved : no excellencies, where prudish cant and dull regularity are absent, can preserve it from the contempt and abhorrence of the multitude. It is evidently not difficult to imagine an instance in which the most elevated genius shall be recompensed with neglect. Mediocrity alone seems unvaryingly to escape rebuke and obloquy, it accom[m]odates its attempts to the spirit of the age, which has produced it, and adopts with mimic effrontery the cant of the day and hour for which alone it lives.

We think that 'the Memoirs of Prince Alexy Haimatoff,' deserves to be regarded as an example of the fact, by the frequency of which, criticism is vindicated from the imputation of futility and impertinence. We do not hesitate to consider this fiction, as the product of a bold and original mind. We hardly remember even [ever ?] to have seen surpassed the subtle delicacy of imagination, by which the manifest distinctions of character, and form are seized and pictured in colours, that almost make nature more

beautiful than herself. The vulgar observe no resemblances or discrepancies, but such as are gross
and glaring. The science of mind to which history,
poetry, biography serve as the materials, consists in
the discernment of shades and distinctions where the
unenlightened discover nothing but a shapeless and
unmeaning mass. The faculty for this discernment
distinguishes genius from dulness. There are passages
in the production before us, which afford instances of
just and rapid intuition belonging only to intelligences, that possess this faculty in no ordinary
degree. As a composition the book is far from faultless. Its abruptness and angularities do not appear to
have received the slightest polish or correction. The
author has written with fervour but has disdained to
revise at leisure. These errors are the errors of youth
and genius and the fervid impatience of sensibilities
impetuously disburthening their fulness. The author
is proudly negligent of connecting the incidents of his
tale. It appears more like the recorded day dream
of a poet, not unvisited by the sublimest and most
lovely visions, than the tissue of a romance skilfully
interwoven for the purpose of maintaining the interest
of the reader, and conducting his sympathies by
dramatic gradations to the denouement. It is, what
it professes to be, a memoir, not a novel. Yet its
claims to the former appellation are established, only
by the impatience and inexperience of the author,

who, possessing in an eminent degree, the higher
qualifications of a novelist, we had almost said a poet,
has neglected the number by which that success
would probably have been secured, which, in this
instance, merit[s] of a far nobler stamp, have unfortunately failed to acquire. Prince Alexy is by no means
an unnatural, although no common character. We
think we can discern his counterpart in Alfieri's[1]
delineation of himself. The same propensities, the
same ardent devotion to his purposes, the same
chivalric and unproductive attachment to unbounded
liberty, characterizes both. We are inclined to doubt
whether the author has not attributed to his hero, the
doctrines of universal philanthropy in a spirit of
profound and almost unsearchable irony : at least he
appears biassed by no peculiar principles, and it were
perhaps an insoluble inquiry whether any, and if any,
what moral truth he designed to illustrate by his tale.
Bruhle, the tutor of Alexy, is a character delineated
with consummate skill ; the power of intelligence and
virtue over external deficiencies, is forcibly exemplified. The calmness, patience and magnanimity
of this singular man, are truly rare and admirable :
his disinterestedness, his equanimity, his irresistible
gentleness form a finished and delightful portrait. But we cannot regard his commendation to
his pupil to indulge in promiscuous concubinage

---

[1] *Alfieri's* in the original.

without horror and detestation. The author appears
to deem the loveless intercourse of brutal appetite,
a venial offence against delicacy and virtue! he
asserts that a transient connection with a cultivated
female, may contribute to form the heart without
essentially vitiating the sensibilities. It is our duty
to protest against so pernicious and disgusting an
opinion. No man can rise pure from the poisonous
embraces of a prostitute, or sinless from the desolated
hopes of a confiding heart. Whatever may be the
claims of chastity, whatever the advantages of simple
and pure affections, these ties, these benefits are of
equal obligation to either sex.[1] Domestic relations
depend for their integrity upon a complete reciprocity
of duties. But the author himself has in the adventure of the sultana, Debesh-Sheptuti afforded a most
impressive and tremendous allegory of the cold
blooded and malignant selfishness of sensuality.

We are incapacitated by the unconnected and
vague narrative from forming an analysis of the incidents, they would consist indeed, simply of a
catalogue of events, and which, divested of the aërial
tinge of genius might appear trivial and common.
We shall content ourselves, therefore with selecting
some passages calculated to exemplify the peculiar
powers of the author. The following description of
the simple and interesting Rosalie is in the highest

---

[1] *Six* in the original.

style of delineation, ' Her hair was unusually black,
she truly had raven locks, the same glossiness, the
same varying shade, the same mixture of purple
and sable for which the plumage of the raven is remarkable, were found in the long elastic tresses
depending from her head and covering her shoulders.
Her complexion was dark and clear : the colours which
composed the brown that dyed her smooth skin, were
so well mixed, that not one blot, not one varied tinge
injured its brightness, and when the blush of animation
or of modesty flushed her cheek, the tint was so rare,
that could a painter have dipped his pencil in it,
that single shade would have rendered him immortal.
The bone above her eye was sharp, and beautifully
curved ; much as I have admired the wonderful
properties of curves, I am convinced that their most
stupendous properties collected, would fall far short
of that magic line. The eyebrow was pencilled with
extreme nicety ; in the centre it consisted of the
deepest shade of black, at the edges it was hardly
perceptible, and no man could have been hardy enough
to have attempted to define the precise spot at which
it ceased : in short the velvet drapery of the eyebrow
was only to be rivalled by the purple of the long
black eyelashes that terminated the ample curtain.
Rosalie's eyes were large and full ; they appeared at
a distance uniformly dark, but upon close inspection
the innumerable strokes of various hues of infinite

fineness and endless variety drawn in concentric circles behind the pellucid chrystal, filled the mind with wonder and admiration, and could only be the work of infinite power directed by infinite wisdom.'

Alexy's union with Aür-Ahebeh the Circassian slave is marked by circumstances of deep pathos, and the sweetest tenderness of sentiment. The description of his misery and madness at her death, deserves to be remarked as affording evidence of an imagination vast, profound and full of energy.

' Alexy, who gained the friendship, perhaps the love of the native Rosalie : the handsome Haimatoff, the philosophic Haimatoff, the haughty Haimatoff, Haimatoff the gay, the witty, the accomplished, the bold hunter, the friend of liberty, the chivalric lover of all that is feminine, the hero, the enthusiast : see him now, that is he, mark him ! he appears in the shades of evening, he stalk[s] as a spectre, he has just risen from the damps of the charnel house ; see, the dews still hang on his forehead.   He will vanish at cock-crowing, he never heard the song of the lark, nor the busy hum of men ; the sun's rays never warmed him, the pale moonbeam alone shews his unearthly figure, which is fanned by the wing of the owl, which scarce obstructs the slow flight of the droning beetle,[1] or of the drowsy bat. Mark him ! he stops, his lean arms are crossed on his bosom ; he is bowed to the earth, his sunken eye gazes from its deep cavity on vacuity, as the toad skulking in the corner of a sepulchre, peeps with malignity through the circum[am]-bient gloom.   His cheek is hollow ; the glowing tints of his

---

[1] *beatle* in the original.

complexion, which once resembled the autumnal sunbeam
on the autumnal beech, are gone, the cadaverous yellow,
the livid hue have usurped their place, the sable honours of
his head have perished, they once waved in the wind like the
jetty pinions of the raven, the skull is only covered by the
shrivelled skin, which the rook views wistfully, and calls to
her young ones. His gaunt bones start from his wrinkled
garments, his voice is deep, hollow, sepulchral[;] it is the
voice which wakes the dead, he has long held converse
with the departed. He attempts to walk he knows not
whither, his legs totter under him, he falls, the boys hoot
him, the dogs bark at him, he hears them not, he sees
them not.—Rest there, Alexy, it beseemeth thee, thy bed is
the grave, thy bride is the worm, yet once thou stoodest
erect, thy cheek was flushed with joyful ardour, thy eye
blazing told what thy head conceived, what thy heart felt,
thy limbs were vigour and activity, thy bosom expanded
with pride, ambition, and desire, every nerve thrilled to
feel, every muscle swelled to execute.

'Haimatoff, the blight has tainted thee, thou ample
roomy web of life, whereon were traced the gaudy characters,
the gay embroidery of pleasure, how has the moth battened
on thee ; Haimatoff, how has the devouring flame scorched
the plains, once yellow with the harvest ! the simoon, the
parching breath of the desert, has swept over the laughing
plains, the carpet of verdure rolled away at its approach, and
has bared amid desolation. Thou stricken deer, thy leather
coat, thy dappled hide hangs loose upon thee, it was a deadly
arrow, how has it wasted thee, thou scathed oak, how has the
red lightning drank thy sap : Haimatoff, Haimatoff, eat thy
soul with vexation. Let the immeasurable ocean roll between thee and pride : you must not dwell together.' P. 129.

The episode of Viola is affecting, natural, and beautiful. We do not ever remember to have seen the unforgiving fastidiousness of family honor more awfully illustrated. After the death of her lover, Viola still expects that he will esteem, still cherishes the delusion that he is not lost to her for ever.

'She used frequently to go to the window to look for him, or walk in the Park to meet him, but without the least impatience, at his delay. She learnt a new tune, or a new song to amuse him, she stood behind the door to startle him as he entered, or disguised herself to surprise him.'

The character of Mary, deserves, we think, to be considered as the only complete failure in the book. Every other female whom the author has attempted to describe is designated by an individuality peculiarly marked and true. They constitute finished portraits of whatever is eminently simple, graceful, gentle, or disgustingly atrocious and vile. Mary alone is the miserable parasite of fashion, the tame slave of drivelling and drunken folly, the cold hearted coquette, the lying and meretricious prude. The means employed to gain this worthless prize corresponds exactly with its worthlessness. Sir Fulke[1] Hildebrand is a strenuous tory, Alexy, on his arrival in England professes himself inclined to the principles of the whig party, finding that the Baronet had sworn that his daughter should never

---

[1] *Eulke* in the original.

marry a whig, he sacrifices his principles and with inconceivable effrontery thus palliates his apostacy and falsehood.

'The prejudices of the Baronet, were strong in proportion as they were irrational. I resolved rather to humour than to thwart them. I contrived to be invited to dine in company with him; I always proposed the health of the minister, I introduced politics and defended the tory party in long speeches, I attended clubs and public dinners of that interest. I do not know whether this conduct was justifiable; it may certainly be excused when the circumstances of my case are duly considered. I would tear myself in pieces, if I suspected that I could be guilty of the slightest falsehood or prevarication; (see Lord Chesterfield's letters for the courtier-like distinction between simulation and dissimulation,) but there was nothing of that sort here. I was of no party, consequently, I could not be accused of deserting any one. I did not defend the injustice of any body of men, I did not detract from the merits of any virtuous character. I praised what was laudable in the tory party, and blamed what was reprehensible in the whigs: I was silent with regard to whatever was culpable in the former or praiseworthy in the latter. The stratagem was innocent, which injured no one, and which promoted the happiness of two individuals, especially of the most amiable woman the world ever knew.'

An instance of more deplorable perversity of the human understanding we do not recollect ever to have witnessed. It almost persuades us to believe that scepticism or indifference concerning certain

sacred truths may occasionally produce a subtlety
of sophism, by which the conscience of the criminal
may be bribed to overlook his crime.

Towards the conclusion of this strange and
powerful performance it must be confessed that
aliquando bonus dormitat Homerus. The adventure
of the Eleutheri, although the sketch of a profounder
project, is introduced and concluded with unintelligible abruptness. Bruhle dies, purposely as it
should seem that his pupil may renounce the romantic sublimity of his nature, and that his inauspicious
union and prostituted character, might be exempt
from the censure of violated friendship. Numerous
indications of profound and vigorous thought are
scattered over even the most negligently compacted
portions of the narrative. It is an unweeded garden
where nightshade is interwoven with sweet jessamine,
and the most delicate spices of the east, peep over
struggling stalks of rank and poisonous hemlock.

In the delineation of the more evanescent feelings
and uncommon instances of strong and delicate
passion we conceive the author to have exhibited
new and unparalleled powers. He has noticed some
peculiarities of female character, with a delicacy
and truth singularly exquisite. We think that the
interesting subject of sexual relations requires for
its successful development the application of a mind
thus organised and endowed. Yet even here how

great the deficiencies ; this mind must be pure from
the fashionable superstitions of gallantry, must be
exempt from the sordid feelings which with blind
idolatry worship [1] the image and blaspheme the
deity, reverence the type, and degrade the reality
of which it is an emblem.

We do not hesitate to assert that the author of
this volume is a man of ability. His great though
indisciplinable energies and fervid rapidity of conception embodies scenes and situations, and of
passions affording inexhaustible food for wonder
and delight. The interest is deep and irresistible.
A moral enchanter seems to have conjured up the
shapes of all that is beautiful and strange to suspend
the faculties in fascination and astonishment.

---

[1] *Worships* in the original.

PROF. DOWDEN

ON

SHELLEY'S REVIEW OF

HOGG'S

"Memoirs of Prince Alexy Haimatoff."

FROM

" Some Early Writings of Shelley."

BY PROFESSOR DOWDEN.[1]

In the *Critical Review* for December, 1814,[2] appeared an article of considerable length reviewing a duodecimo volume published by the Hookhams in the preceding year :—" Memoirs of Prince Alexy Haimatoff: Translated from the original Latin MSS. under the immediate inspection of the Prince. By John Brown, Esqre." The writer of this imaginary autobiography was Shelley's friend Thomas Jefferson Hogg, and the writer of the review was no other than Shelley.

From Edinburgh, on November 26, 1813, Shelley wrote a letter to Hogg, printed in the second volume

---

[1] From *The Contemporary Review*, September, 1884, pp. 383-396. —T. J. W.

[2] Vol. vi. No. vi. art. vii. pp. 566-574.—T. J. W.

of " The Life of Shelley " [pp. 480-482], from which
the following is an extract :—

"Your novel is now printed.   I need not assure you
with what pleasure this extraordinary and animated tale is
perused by me.   Every one to whom I have shown it agrees
with me in admitting that it bears indisputable marks of a
singular and original genius.   Write more like this.   Delight us again with a character so natural and energetic as
Alexy—vary again the scene with an uncommon combination
of the most natural and simple circumstances : but do not
persevere in writing after you grow weary of your toil ;
' aliquando bonus dormitat Homerus ; ' and the swans and
the Eleutherarchs are proofs that you were a little sleepy."

No explanation of this passage, no comment on it,
was vouchsafed by Hogg; but the allusion to
" Eleutherarchs " may perhaps have reminded some
readers of a paragraph in Peacock's satirical extrava-
ganza "Nightmare Abbey," in which he describes
how young Scythrop—a fantastic counterfeit of the
youthful Shelley—became troubled with a passion
for reforming the world :—

"He built many castles in the air, and peopled them with
secret tribunals, and bands of illuminati, who were always
the imaginary instruments of his projected regeneration of
the human species.   As he intended to institute a perfect
republic, he invested himself with absolute sovereignty over
these mystical dispensers of liberty.   He slept with horrid
mysteries under his pillow, *and dreamed of venerable
Eleutherarchs* and ghastly confederates holding midnight
conversation in subterranean caves."

Every one, Shelley assures his friend, admits that the tale bears "indisputable marks of a singular and original genius." A few days previously, the publisher, Hookham, had written in a flutter to Hogg, because the editor of the *Quarterly Review* had sent for a copy of the book, of which Hookham expected to be able to give a good account before long :—

"That Prince Haimatoff is really published the delivery of six copies of his memoirs will prove; he has been sent to the booksellers this morning only [November 8, 1813]. The editor of the *Quarterly Review* sent for a copy on Saturday last : there is a mystery in this which I shall be very glad to have explained: perhaps you can elucidate it. . . . . I have a presentiment that His Serene Highness will shortly be in very general request." [1]

Hookham's presentiment was not verified. The book seems to have dropped still-born from the press; it was unnoticed by the reviewers; no copy of the Prince's Memoirs is to be found in the British Museum Library ; [2] and it is only through the kindness of Mr. Hogg's daughter that I have been enabled to see a copy—the sole copy of which, after some research, I

[1] From an unpublished letter which I have been permitted to use by Mr. Hogg's daughter, Mrs Lonsdale.—E. D.
[2] The British Museum does possess a copy of the book, but this was unknown to Professor Dowden at the time—September, 1884—he wrote this article.—T. J. W.

have heard tidings. It was the entire neglect of a work which he conceived to be " the product of a bold and original mind," that moved Shelley to assume the part of critic ; and in the opening paragraphs of his article he considers whether the indifference of the public is in itself sufficient to condemn a writer of genius and his work :—

" Is the suffrage of mankind the legitimate criterion of intellectual energy? Are complaints of the aspirants to literary fame to be considered as the honourable disappoint- ment of neglected genius, or the sickly impatience of a dreamer miserably self-deceived? The most illustrious ornaments of the annals of the human race have been stigmatised by the contempt and abhorrence of entire communities of man ; but this injustice arose out of some temporary superstition, some partial interest, some national doctrine ; a glorious redemption awaited their remembrance. There is, indeed, nothing so remarkable in the contempt of the ignorant for the enlightened ; the vulgar pride of folly delights to triumph upon mind. This is an intelligible process ; the infamy or ingloriousness that can be thus explained detracts nothing from the beauty of virtue or the sublimity of genius. But what does utter obscurity express? If the public do not advert, even in censure, to a performance, has that performance already received its condemnation?

"The result of this controversy is important to the ingenuous critic. His labours are indeed miserably worth- less, if their objects may invariably be attained before their application. He should know the limits of his prerogative.

He should not be ignorant whether it is his duty to promulgate the decisions of others, or to cultivate his taste and judgment that he may be enabled to render a reason of his own.

"Circumstances the least connected with intellectual nature have contributed, for a certain period, to retain in obscurity the most memorable specimens of human genius. The author refrains perhaps from introducing his production to the world with all the pomp of empirical bibliopolism. A sudden tide in the affairs of men may make the neglect or contradiction of some insignificant doctrine a badge of obscurity and discredit; those even who are exempt from the action of these absurd predilections are necessarily in an indirect manner affected by their influence. It is perhaps the product of an imagination daring and undisciplined; the majority of readers, ignorant and disdaining toleration, refuse to pardon a neglect of common rules; their canons of criticism are carelessly infringed; it is less religious than a charity sermon, less methodical and cold than a French tragedy, where all the unities are preserved; no excellencies, where prudish cant and dull regularity are absent, can preserve it from the contempt and abhorrence of the multitude. It is evidently not difficult to imagine an instance in which the most elevated genius shall be recompensed with neglect. Mediocrity alone seems unvaryingly to escape rebuke and obloquy; it accommodates its attempts to the spirit of the age which has produced it, and adopts with mimic effrontery the cant of the day and hour for which alone it lives."

In later days when Shelley had tested the feeling of the public with works of his own, and found but little

response to his impassioned utterances, such reflec-
tions as these may have recurred to his mind with
added force.   In the instance of Prince Alexy
Haimatoff he does not hesitate to record his solitary
vote in its favour against the unjust majority :—

" We think that the memoirs of Prince Alexy Haimatoff
deserve to be regarded as an example of the fact, by the
frequency of which criticism is vindicated from the imputation of futility and impertinence. We do not hesitate to
consider this fiction as the product of a bold and original
mind. We hardly remember ever to have seen surpassed
the subtle delicacy of imagination, by which the manifest
distinctions of character and form are seized and pictured
in colours, that almost make Nature more beautiful than
herself. The vulgar observe no resemblances or discrepancies
but such as are gross and glaring. The science of mind, to
which history, poetry, biography serve as the materials,
consists in the discernment of shades and distinctions,
where the unenlightened discover nothing but a shapeless
and unmeaning mass. The faculty for this discernment distinguishes genius from dulness.[1] There are passages in
the production before us, which afford instances of just and
rapid intuition belonging only to intelligences that possess
this faculty in no ordinary degree. As a composition the
book is far from faultless. Its abruptness and angularities

------

[1] Compare Shelley's words respecting himself in a letter to Godwin,
December 11, 1817 :—" I am formed, if for anything not in common
with the herd of mankind, to apprehend minute and remote distinctions
of feeling, whether relative to external nature or the living beings
which surround us, and to communicate the conceptions which result
from considering either the moral or the material universe as a
whole."—E. D.

do not appear to have received the slightest polish or correction. The author has written with fervour, but has disdained to revise at leisure. These errors are the errors of youth and genius, and the fervid impatience of sensibilities impetuously unburthening their fulness. The author is proudly negligent of connecting the incidents of his tale. It appears more like the recorded day-dream of a poet, not unvisited by the sublimest and most lovely visions, than the tissue of a romance skilfully interwoven for the purpose of maintaining the interest of the reader, and conducting his sympathies by dramatic gradations to the denouement. It is what it professes to be, a memoir, not a novel. Yet its claims to the former appellation are established only by the impatience and inexperience of the author, who, possessing in an eminent degree the higher qualifications of a novelist, we had almost said a poet, has neglected the number by which that success would probably have been secured, which, in this instance, merits of a far nobler stamp have unfortunately failed to acquire."

Readers of Hogg's "Life of Shelley" think of the writer as a clever man of the world, witty and ingenious, a hater of crotchets and abstractions and theory-mongers, an enjoyer of the good things of life, and, above all, of a good story—in brief, as the reverse in almost every way of "the divine poet," whom he applauds while smiling at him—helpless angel with awkward wings—the touch of mundane disdain broadening visibly at times on the applauder's lips. " Hogg despised poetry," says Trelawny, " he thought it all nonsense, and barely tolerated Shakespeare."

But this surely is an exaggeration; at least it is
certain that in earlier days Hogg was a zealous
student of literature, and cared for Plato and the
Greek dramatists as much as for Blackstone or Coke.
In truth, the Thomas Jefferson Hogg, who was
Shelley's comrade at Oxford, while having within
him a potential man of the world, to be afterwards
developed by circumstance, owned much more in
common with Shelley, and was in every way much
more of a romantic person than readers of his " Life
of Shelley " may be disposed to admit. He wrote
poetry; he planned romances; to his fellow-students
he seemed a youth of high intellectual powers, but
singular and wilful in his bearing and habits; and
we must put to his credit the fine indiscretion with
which he came forward to claim an equal share in
the responsibility incurred by Shelley as the author,
or assumed author, of " The Necessity of Atheism."
It would be interesting if we could get some account of
" Leonora," a fiction partly founded on a piteous tale
of real life, the joint production, it is said, of the two
inseparable Oxford friends, and in great part in type,
when tidings of their expulsion from University
College alarmed the Abingdon printer, King, in
whose hands was the manuscript, and placed an
obstacle in the way of the intended publication.
"Leonora" has probably disappeared beyond recovery.
We must rest content with making the acquaintance

of Hogg as romancer, and of Shelley as his re-
viewer, at a date three years and a half subsequent
to the scene in the common room of University
College, on Lady-day, 1811.

Prince Alexy Haimatoff was born at St. Peters-
burg, of illustrious parents, who, however, made a
secret of his birth. At the age of five or six he was
sent to Lausanne, there to be educated under the care
of an elderly French clergyman, Monsieur Gothon.
This venerable pedagogue made amends for his stern
and forbidding aspect, and a plainness of manners
bordering on coarseness, by his profound skill in
ancient literature, his passionate love of the abstruser
sciences, and the stern and philosophic regard with
which he watched over the best interests of his pupils.
Haimatoff, condemned to physical inactivity by
weakness of an ankle, yet of a disposition eager,
glowing, and insatiable, became an enthusiastic
student, and at the age of fifteen was his master's
favourite pupil. In two things only was he deficient
—he had acquired none of those habits of prompt
and decisive action which his associates had formed
in their boyish sports and in the use of arms; and
his heart was as little exercised as were his limbs.
The tall, slight, effeminate student lacked manly
vigour and courage, yet he despised all women as
the intellectual inferiors of such beings as his master
and himself. Before long one of these defects was

remedied, and Alexy had found an Egeria to be his instructress and inspirer. Rosalie, a distant relation of M. Gothon, a charming girl of seventeen, who had lately lost her parents, was placed by the old schoolmaster, somewhat indiscreetly, at the head of his table, and made mistress of his house. I spare my reader the author's description of the charms of Rosalie, several pages in length, although it is declared by Shelley to be " in the highest style of delineation." One particular only shall here be noted—the peculiar beauty of Rosalie's eyes: " Rosalie's eyes were large and full : they appeared at a distance uniformly dark; but upon a closer inspection the innumerable strokes of various hues of infinite fineness and endless variety, drawn in concentric circles behind the pellucid crystal, filled the mind with wonder and admiration." Can Shelley, who quotes at length the description of Rosalie, have had some vague memory of this passage, when long afterwards he wrote the lines of Prometheus Unbound, in which Asia describes the eyes of her sister Panthea :

> " Thine eyes are like the deep, blue, boundless heaven,
> Contracted to two circles underneath
> Their long fine lashes ; dark, far, measureless,
> Orb within orb, and line thro' line inwoven." [1]

---

[1] In Hogg's description of Haimatoff one touch seems to be taken direct from Shelley's person : "My hands were very small and my head remarkable for its roundness and diminutive size." Compare " Life of Shelley," i. p. 328 : " The air of his little round hat upon his little round head was troubled and peculiar."—E. D.

The more Prince Alexy sees of Rosalie the less reason has he to be satisfied with his theory of the inferiority of woman to man. True, she cares not for Aristotle's ethics or rhetoric ; she learns from a mountain mist more than she can learn from all the geometrical diagrams of M. Gothon and his pupil ; she does not read poetry, for it seems as if she already knew whatever it has to say; yet by some strange intuitive energies of her mind, she has gained more of true wisdom than can be found in the most cultivated intellects. Rosalie is introduced into Hogg's romance only to be withdrawn as soon as she has quickened and aroused the heart of Haimatoff; she dies, and her disconsolate lover is called away from Lausanne by his old kinsman, Baron Groutermann, master of a venerable German castle in which feudal and military ideas are the ruling powers. Here Haimatoff is initiated into the arts of war, and shaking off his physical weakness, becomes ere long a keen and desperate sportsman, a frantic follower of the chase. But intellectual pursuits are not neglected, and a tutor for the young Prince is secured in the person of Mr. Frederic Bruhle, a strange and remarkable being, who henceforth exercises a dominant influence over Haimatoff's character and fortunes :—

" He was about five feet in height, crooked and club-footed ; his head was high and peaked ; he squinted ; his hair was long and lank, his complexion sallow, and his

D

mouth awry. . . . . His manners, however, were mild, attentive, and perfectly unassuming; he adopted, rather than gave, the subject of conversation; he expressed great respect for the opinion of every person, and, if his own sentiments were different, he softened the apparent without diminishing the real difference, and conveyed what was diametrically opposite in terms at once so gentle and so powerful as often to convince and never to offend. He carefully avoided the appearance of being striking, so as never to excite jealousy and opposition; he never wounded, but, on the contrary, occasionally flattered self-love, so as imperceptibly, by mild insinuation, to wind himself into the hearts of all who knew him."

This amazing deformity, Bruhle, is unrivalled in his mastery of Latin; skilled in music; a painter; a profound adept in all sciences; and, to crown the wonders, he will accept no salary. It is not until long after this first acquaintance with Bruhle that Haimatoff discovers in his master a member of a secret society of Illuminati, advocates of unbounded political liberty, materialists in philosophy, and presided over by the supreme Eleutherarch. Shelley's remarks on the characters of pupil and teacher, and on Bruhle's licentious wisdom are not without interest. Amid the animalisms of young Oxford Shelley remained, says his wife, "of the purest morals;" "the purity and sanctity of his life," declares Hogg, "were most conspicuous."

"Alexy is by no means an unnatural although no common character. We think we can discern his counterpart in

Alfieri's delineation of himself. The same propensities, the same ardent devotion to his purposes, the same chivalric and unproductive attachment to unbounded liberty, characterises both. We are inclined to doubt whether the author has not attributed to his hero the doctrines of universal philanthropy in a spirit of profound and almost unsearchable irony : at least, he appears biassed by no peculiar principles, and it were perhaps an insoluble inquiry whether any, and if any, what moral truth he designed to illustrate by his tale. Bruhle, the tutor of Alexy, is a character delineated with consummate skill ; the power of intelligence and virtue over external deficiencies is forcibly exemplified. The calmness, patience, and magnanimity of this singular man are truly rare and admirable ; his disinterestedness, his equanimity, his irresistible gentleness, form a finished and delightful portrait. But we cannot regard his commendation to his pupil to indulge in promiscuous concubinage without horror and detestation. . . . . Whatever may be the claims of chastity, whatever the advantages of pure and simple affections, these ties, these benefits are of equal obligation to either sex. Domestic relations depend for their integrity upon a complete reciprocity of duties. But the author himself has in the adventure of the 'Sultana Debesh Sheptuti,' afforded a most impressive and tremendous allegory of the cold-blooded and malignant selfishness of sensuality."

—

Baron Groutermann, Alexy's aged kinsman, having died, the Prince, accompanied by his tutor Bruhle, sets forth upon his travels. They visit Athens, and one night, while climbing the steep of the Parthenon, Alexy, unperceived, is spectator of a moonlight dance

performed by ten Grecian maidens, who chant while
evolving their slow and solemn movements.   At
Constantinople, he is inveigled by the arts of the
Sultana into the Seraglio; but escapes, and finds his
way back to the faithful Bruhle.   And now he wins
the love of a fair Circassian slave—a timid and
trembling dove, who yet unites an exquisite vivacity
with her gentleness.   The slave, Aür-Ahibah, becomes
Alexy's wife; happy years go by, made happier by
the birth of two sons ; when fate strikes at the heart
of all this joy—the babes are seized with small-pox
and die, and their mother quickly follows them to
the grave. Alexy is distracted, and it is not long
before his madness gives place to a deep and enduring
melancholy.   At length he resumes his travels in
company with Bruhle.   They spend some months at
Rome, shocked at "the grinding oppression of the
Church, the spiritual despotism of the ecclesiastics,"
delighted with the recollections summoned up by the
ruins of the ancient city.   At Florence, the Prince
meets with an old schoolfellow of the Lausanne days,
and is obliged to act as his second in a fatal affair of
honour.   " We do not ever remember," writes Shelley,
" to have seen the unforgiving fastidiousness of family
honour more awfully illustrated."   At length Bruhle
thinks the time has come for disclosing to Haimatoff
the end towards which his education has been directed.
They travel north, and arrive at an old university

town of Germany. The description of the University
—really the centre of a secret society of the Eleutheri
—represents Hogg's romance at its best :—

"When we arrived at the University, we were ushered into
a spacious hall, floored and wainscotted with black oak ; the
roof was of the same materials, most elaborately carved with
armorial bearings and grotesque figures ; the windows were
filled with painted glass, and the walls were hung with portraits of benefactors and the most eminent members of the
Society ; the whole of the apartment was in the style of the
most noble of college halls. The room was lighted by a
large fire, abundantly piled with logs of wood. Several
venerable old men were seated upon benches at a little
distance from the fire ; they rose to receive us, and em-
bracing Bruhle in the most affectionate manner, expressed
their satisfaction in welcoming him again. My friend then
presented me ; I was received with a simple dignity, which
charmed me. I had never witnessed manners at once so
free from all restraint, and so dignified. It called to my
mind what I had read of the noble plainness of the Romans,
entirely devoid of all ceremony, and so stately as to inspire
the most profound veneration. I contemplated their wrinkled
faces, replete with the most profound knowledge, and the
most amiable complacency ; their sunken eyes, in which the
fires of genius were tempered by the experience of age ;
their figures gracefully bending under the weight of years ;
the plain neatness of their garments."

They speak of the dignity, the liberty, the happiness
of man, and hint at the necessity of a general reform.
Above the rest, one of the fathers, who sits shaded in

the chimney-corner, impresses Haimatoff by his appearance: " He was a tall man; his arms were folded upon his breast; he appeared about fourscore years of age; his head was bald, his complexion sallow, his nose large and prominent, and of the finest Roman form; his eyes small but dark and piercing; they were rivetted upon me, as if they could penetrate my inmost soul. He was motionless as a statue." This is no other than the Eleutherarch, the principal of the University. Next day he explains to Haimatoff the purpose of their Society—to restore to man his natural rights, to banish oppression, to break the bonds, to shake off the yoke of slavery. A three years' noviciate precedes admission into the Society of the Eleutheri, which by special permission is reduced to one year in the case of Haimatoff. After a public discourse to prove that the soul is material, and that death is complete annihilation, an eternal sleep, the Eleutherarch conducts Haimatoff to the cathedral to watch, as part of the initiatory rites, night-long and alone beside a corpse wrapt in graveclothes and extended on the bier; in his right hand the novice holds a dagger, in his left a skull. Moonlight vaguely entering the church, and sad and solemn organ strains add awe and wonder to the ceremony. Presently a strange and sudden noise is heard, like the flapping of large wings, and white forms are discerned floating aloft in the air, and waving their spectral pinions. At length the welcome morning dawns and ends these terrors of the night. The novice is brought before the Eleutherarch, to whom he makes confession of all the thoughts which had passed through his brain during the night, and these confessions are placed among the archives of the Society. Three months of solitary confinement follow these rites in the cathedral : " it is of admirable use," observes the Eleutherarch, "in condensing the mind." On being released from his prison, Haimatoff is next required to set down in writing an exactly truthful account of his past life ; and then, and not till then, is he instructed in the secret language spoken by the Eleutheri. Finally, when the year of probation has expired, he is invited to take the oath of obedience to the Eleutherarch and Eleutheri in council. Its terms are so absolute that he starts back in alarm, and in a sudden recoil of horror is about to strike the venerable president of the Society with his dagger. " With a serene countenance he bared his breast, and pointing to his heart, said, ·' Strike there, Alexy ; thy blow will then be effectual.' I trembled in every limb. ' Nay, if thy hand is unsteady, let me guide it,' he continued, taking hold of my hand and raising it as if to strike. The dagger fell to the ground." Alexy is banished for twelve months to England. And here, while one evening seeing Garrick in " Richard the Third,"

Alexy's attention is attracted by "a young female"
in the front row of the boxes—the daughter of Sir
Fulke Hildebrand, the Mary who saves him from
further thought of Eleutheri or Eleutherarchs, and
who, after various trials and difficulties have been
overcome, replaces his lost Aür-Ahibah, and becomes
the consolation of his manhood, the support of his
old age.   Mary's father has Tory prejudices, "strong
in proportion as they were irrational."   The astute
Alexy, though a votary of liberty and equality, re-
solves rather to humour than to thwart the Baronet's
foibles : " I contrived to be invited to dine in company
with him.   I always proposed the health of the
minister ; I introduced politics, and defended the
Tory party in long speeches.   I attended clubs and
public dinners in that interest. . . . . The stratagem
was innocent, which injured no one, and which promoted the happiness of two individuals, especially of
the most amiable woman the world ever knew."
With the Prince's marriage to Mary Hildebrand, and
the death of Bruhle a few months later, the memoirs
come to a close.   The fair daughter of the Tory
house does not please Shelley :

"The character of Mary, deserves, we think, to be considered as the only complete failure in the book.   Every
other female whom the author has attempted to describe is
designated by an individuality peculiarly marked and true.
They constitute finished portraits of whatever is eminently

simple, graceful, gentle, or disgustingly atrocious and vile. Mary alone is the miserable parasite of fashion, the tame slave of drivelling and drunken folly, the cold-hearted coquette, the lying and meretricious prude. The means employed to gain this worthless prize corresponds exactly with its worthlessness. Sir Fulke Hildebrand is a strenuous Tory; Alexy on his arrival in England professes himself inclined to the principles of the Whig party; finding that the Baronet had sworn that his daughter should never marry a Whig, he sacrifices his principles, and with inconceivable effrontery thus palliates his apostacy and falsehood. . . . . An instance of more deplorable perversity of the human understanding we do not recollect ever to have witnessed. It almost persuades us to believe that scepticism or indifference concerning certain sacred truths may occasionally produce a subtlety of sophism, by which the conscience of the criminal may be bribed to overlook his crime."

" Aliquando bonus dormitat Homerus," wrote Shelley in his letter to Hogg, of November, 1813, " and the swans and the Eleutherarchs are proofs that you were a little sleepy." The swans of which Shelley speaks thus disrespectfully are those slow-sailing forms of white which Alexy beheld during his midnight watch in the cathedral, birds trained by the Eleutheri to test by their ghost-like apparition the materialistic faith of the novice. In his account of the Society of the Eleutheri, Hogg seems to be indulging in a bad dream after having read a book which was always perused with interest by Shelley —Barruel's " Mémoires pour servir à l'histoire du

Jacobinisme "—let the reader look into the chapters on Spartacus Weishaupt, the founder of Illuminism, and he will see grounds for this conjecture ; and Bruhle, in capturing and preparing Alexy for the Society, plays the part of the Abbé Barruel's illuminé, bearing the title of "le Frère insinuant ou l'Enrôleur." A year later than his letter to Hogg, Shelley, when writing his article for the *Critical Review*, was still of the same opinion respecting the swans and the Eleutherarch :—

"Towards the conclusion of this strange and powerful performance it must be confessed that *aliquando bonus dormitat Homerus.* The adventure of the Eleutheri, although the sketch of a profounder project, is introduced and concluded with unintelligible abruptness. Bruhle dies, purposely, as it should seem, that his pupil may renounce the romantic sublimity of his nature, and that his inauspicious union and prostituted character might be exempt from the censure of violated friendship."

Summing up his judgment upon the romance as a whole, Shelley writes, at the close of his review :—

"Numerous indications of profound and vigorous thought are scattered over even the most negligently compacted portions of the narrative. It is an unweeded garden, where nightshade is interwoven with sweet jessamine, and the most delicate spices of the East peep over struggling stalks of rank and poisonous hemlock.

"In the delineation of the more evanescent feelings and uncommon instances of strong and delicate passion we conceive the author to have exhibited new and unparalleled powers. He has noticed some peculiarities of female character with a delicacy and truth singularly exquisite. We think the interesting subject of sexual relations requires for its successful development the application of a mind thus organised and endowed. Yet even here how great the deficiencies ; this mind must be pure from the fashionable superstitions of gallantry, must be exempt from the sordid feelings which, with blind idolatry, worship the image and blaspheme the deity, reverence the type and degrade the reality of which it is an emblem.

" We do not hesitate to assert that the author of this volume is a man of ability. His great though indisciplinable energies, and fervid rapidity of conception embodies scenes and situations and of passions (*sic*) affording inexhaustible food for wonder and delight. The interest is deep and irresistible. A moral enchanter seems to have conjured up the shapes of all that is beautiful and strange to suspend the faculties in fascination and astonishment."

The general verdict on Hogg's romance was not reversed by Shelley's extravagant eulogy, and Hogg himself probably accepted the general verdict as just. Shelley, in 1814, was far from being a trustworthy critic of books or men. A person, a poem, or a tale which stimulated his imagination and moved his feelings was at once idealised by Shelley, and was viewed through a golden vapour which magnified the object it half concealed. It was indeed so with Shelley to the close, but as his mind matured, he conferred its splendour more and more often upon

things which are in themselves truly admirable and
splendid.

Shelley was at work on his review of " Prince Alexy
Haimatoff" on November 16, 1814, and did not cease
to write until long past midnight. He resumed his
work early next day, and then turned for relief to
Brockden Brown's romance, "Edgar Huntly." The
December number of the *Critical Review* was
published at the end of the month. On January 3,
1815, Shelley received from Hookham a copy of the
number containing his article. On the evening of
that day Hogg called at Shelley's lodgings, and very
pleasantly sped by the evening hours.

POSTSCRIPT.

I HAVE been asked in what way I was able to identify the article on Hogg's novel in the *Critical Review* as by Shelley. It was thus: in the unpublished journal kept now by Shelley, now by Mary, I read—under the date Wednesday, Nov. 16 [1814]—"Shelley writes his critique till half-past 3 [*i.e.* at night]"; and again,—"Nov. 17—Shelley writes his critique, and then reads *Edgar Huntly* all day." This made me curious. I read again: "Jan. 3rd [1815]. A parcel comes from Hookham—the *Critical Review* which has the critique of *Prince Alexander Haimatoff* in it. . . Hogg comes. A very pleasant evening." Putting the two passages together I guessed that this was the critique written by Shelley in November. I noticed the resemblance between the passage in Shelley's letter to Hogg of Nov. 26, 1813,[1] "'*Aliquando bonus dormitat Homerus*'; and the swans and the Eleutherarchs are proofs that you were a little sleepy," and the passage in the *Review:*[2] "Towards the conclusion

---

[1] See Hogg's *Life of Shelley*, vol. ii. p. 481.—T. J. W.

[2] See *ante*, p. 26.—T. J. W.

of this strange and powerful performance it must be confessed that *aliquando bonus dormitat Homerus.* The adventure of the Eleutheri . . . is introduced and concluded with unintelligible abruptness ; " and the inference was that the writer of the letter and the writer of the article must be one and the same. Other pieces of internal evidence (*e.g.* the reference to *Alfieri's Life*, see pp. 19 and 43, a book which Shelley finished reading on Oct. 22), and the general style of the article left no doubt on my mind.   Perhaps it is right to add that in giving an account of Hogg's novel in the *Contemporary Review* I glided lightly past the voluptuous scenes in the seraglio ; and in quoting from Shelley's article I omitted one of the most remarkable passages—that in which he speaks with horror and detestation of the hired pleasures of sensual appetite.

EDWARD DOWDEN.

Feb. 17, 1886.

You are invited to join

THE SHELLEY SOCIETY.

THE Yearly Subscription (which constitutes Membership) is One Guinea, due every first of January, beginning January 1st, 1886, and should be paid to either the *Chairman of Committee,*

WILLIAM MICHAEL ROSSETTI, Esq.,
5, Endsleigh Gardens, Euston Road, London, N.W.,

or to the *Honorary Secretary,*

SYDNEY E. PRESTON, Esq.,
88, Eaton Place, London, S.W.

This Subscription entitles a Member to one copy of all the Publications of the Society during the current year; to attend, and introduce a friend to, all the Society's Meetings; and to admission for himself and (at least) two friends to the Society's yearly performance of Shelley's *Cenci* or *Hellas.*

The Society's Inaugural Meeting will be held in the Botany Theatre of University College, Gower Street, London, W.C., on Wednesday evening, March 10th, 1886, at 8 P.M., when an address on Shelley will be delivered by the Rev. Stopford A. Brooke, M.A.

The Facsimile Reprint of Shelley's *Adonais* (4to, Pisa, 1821), the Reprint of Shelley's Review of Hogg's *Memoirs of Prince Alexy Haimatoff,* 1814 (never before reprinted), with Prof. Dowden's sketch of Hogg's book, and Part I. of Mr. H. Buxton Forman's *Shelley Bibliography,* will be issued before the Meeting to those Members who have paid their Subscription.

COMMITTEE.

WILLIAM E. A. AXON.
MISS MATHILDE BLIND.
REV. STOPFORD A. BROOKE, M.A.
BERTRAM DOBELL.
ALFRED FORMAN.
H. BUXTON FORMAN.
FREDK. J. FURNIVALL, M.A., PH.D.
(*Treasurer.*)
REV. W. A. HARRISON, M.A.
PROF. A. S. NAPIER, M.A., PH.D.

ROBERT ALFRED POTTS.
WILLIAM MICHAEL ROSSETTI.
(*Chairman.*)
GABRIEL SARRAZIN.
WILLIAM BELL SCOTT.
HENRY SWEET, M.A.
WM. BERNHARD TEGETMEIER.
JOHN TODHUNTER, M.D
A. W. VERRALL, M.A.
THOMAS J. WISE.

Hon. Sec. SYDNEY E. PRESTON, 88, Eaton Place, London, S.W.

LOCAL HONORARY SECRETARIES.

Hackney : E. BERDOE, Tynemouth House, Victoria Park Gate.
Manchester : T. C. ABBOTT, Eastlegh, Queen's Road, Bowdon.
Massachusetts, U.S.A. : Prof. J. M. PIERCE, 4, Kirkland Place, Cambridge.
New York : CHARLES W. FREDERICKSON, 741, Lexington Avenue.
Oxford : GREY H. SKIPWITH (Trinity Coll.), 26, Holywell Street.
Reading : J. J. ROSSITER, 12, Abbot's Walk, Forbury Gardens.
Uxbridge : ALFRED FOUNTAIN, Highfield, Hillingdon.

Bank : London and County, Holborn Branch, 324, High Holborn, W.C.

The Society's Meetings and Papers during its First Session, 1886, will be at University College, Gower Street, at 8 P.M. on Wednesdays

March 10. Inaugural Address on "Shelley," by the Rev. STOPFORD A. BROOKE, M.A.
April 14. "On the Vicissitudes of *Queen Mab*," by H. BUXTON FORMAN.
May 12. "On the Primitiveness of Shelley's View of Nature, its Parallelism with that of the Vedas, and its Contrast with that of Shakspere and other Poets," by HY. SWEET, M.A.
Nov. 10. "Shelley's View of Nature contrasted with Darwin's," by Miss MATHILDE BLIND.
Dec. 15. "A Study of *Prometheus Unbound*," by WILLIAM MICHAEL ROSSETTI.

The Society's Performance of THE CENCI,

Beatrice Cenci	Miss ALMA MURRAY,
Lucretia, Countess Cenci	Miss MAUDE BRENNAN,
Count Cenci	Mr. HERMANN VEZIN,
Orsino	Mr. LEONARD S. OUTRAM,

will be held at a London Theatre on some afternoon early in May, 1886.

If sufficient Subscriptions are received, the Committee will organize a performance of Shelley's *Hellas*, with Dr. W. C. Sellé's music, in November, 1886.

THE SHELLEY SOCIETY.

THIS Society is started to gather the chief admirers of the Poet into a body which will work to do his memory honour, by meeting to discuss his writings, qualities, opinions, life, and doings; by getting his plays acted; by reprinting the rarest of his original editions; by facsimileing such of his MSS. as may be accessible; by compiling a Shelley Lexicon or Concordance; by getting a Shelley Primer published; by generally investigating and illustrating his genius and per- sonality from every side and in every detail; and by extending his influence.

The charm and power of Shelley as poet, essayist, letter- writer and man, are too widely acknowledged to need dwelling on here. No more attractive figure than his beams from the gallery of our literature. The present age is beginning to do justice to the high qualities of his genius, and it is but natural that those men and women who appreciate it should desire to band themselves into a Shelley Society, in which they can commune together and take steps to reach ends which, individually, they could not attain.

One of these is the performance of Shelley's plays. He himself wanted to have his *Cenci* on the stage, with Miss O'NEIL as Beatrice. MACREADY, after he had retired from the boards, declared he would come back to them if he had the chance of playing Count Cenci. Now the Shelley Society can get the play acted early next May. Miss ALMA MURRAY, whose charming performances of Constance and Colombe in Browning's *In a Balcony* and *Colombe's Birthday* have so delighted the Browning Society, has kindly promised to play Beatrice Cenci, and Mr. HERMANN VEZIN and Mr. OUTRAM have been good enough to undertake Count Cenci and Orsino. They will use their influence with other good actors to volunteer for the other parts. *Hellas* may perhaps follow *The Cenci* in November, 1886, or in 1887, as Dr. W. C. Sellé is kindly setting its choruses to music for the Society.

Many points to be discussed in Shelley's works and life, his religion, politics, sociology, views of nature and art, mythology, metre, revisions, development, &c., &c., will occur to every student, as also the need of a reprint of his first editions, of old articles on him, and the facsimileing of his MSS. No one doubts that when a set of Shelley students get together, they will find plenty of work for their Shelley Society to do, and that their Papers and Discussions can be kept clear of any of the old *odium theologicum* and the like. Dispassionate treatment of all Shelley topics is now easy, and is consistent with the entire frankness of expression which the Society will always allow in its Meetings and publications.

It is proposed that the Presidency and Vice-Presidency of the Society be left vacant for the present; but that the Committee consist of Shelley workers, Messrs. W. M. ROSSETTI, H. BUXTON FORMAN, TODHUNTER, B. DOBELL, T. J. WISE, and other students of Shelley, like the Rev. STOPFORD A. BROOKE, the Rev. W. A. HARRISON, Mr. ALFRED FORMAN, Mr. HENRY SWEET (who suggested the formation of a Shelley Society) and Dr. FURNIVALL (the founder of the Society), whose father knew and liked Shelley, as Shelley liked him. The number of the Committee will be twenty. This Committee will manage the Society till December 1886, and then suggest to Members the future Rules and Officers of the Society. (The Society is constituted for ten years only.) The Society's publishers are Messrs. REEVES and TURNER, of 196, Strand, London, W.C.; its printers, Messrs. R. CLAY and SONS, of Bread Street Hill, E.C., and Bungay, Suffolk.

The Society's Meetings will be held at University College, Gower Street, W.C., at 8 P.M., on the second Wednesday in March, April, May, November and December, 1886, &c. The performance of *The Cenci* will be at a London theatre, on some afternoon early in May, 1886.

The Annual Subscription, which constitutes Membership, is One Guinea, due every 1st of January. Members' Names and Subscriptions should be sent at once to W. M. ROSSETTI, Esq., 5, Endsleigh Gardens, London, N.W., or to SYDNEY E. PRESTON, 88, Eaton Place, London, S.W.

8th December, 1885.

The Society's Publications will be issued in Four Series:—

Series I. will consist of the Papers read before the Society, and an Abstract of any which are not printed in full, together with Reports of the Discussions at the Society's Meetings.   The *Abstract* will be edited by the Honorary Secretary, and will contain Shelley "*Notes and Queries*" and ' News,' for both of which, contributions from Members are desired.

Series II. will be a set of Facsimile Reprints of all the rarest works of Shelley, with full bibliographical Notices.   Of these a list will be found on page 6.

Series III. will consist of Reprints of the most important *Magazine Articles* on Shelley and his Works :

§ 1. *Biographical*, beginning with Hogg's seven important articles on "Shelley at Oxford," &c., in *The New Monthly Magazine*, 1832 and 1833.

§ 2. *Contemporary Criticisms* of Shelley's Works.   (The abusive tone of most of these constitutes their main interest to Shelley students.)

§ 3. *Critical Articles* in later periodicals on Shelley and his Works. Though these will be mainly from journals of the last ten years (see the list on page 8), yet such Reviews as those of Shelley's *Posthumous Poems* in *The Edinburgh Review* of July 1824 (vol. xl. pp. 494-514, by Hazlitt), in the *Quarterly* of June 1826 (vol. xxxiv. pp. 148-153), in the *Metropolitan Quarterly Magazine* (No. 3), 1826, and *The Mirror* (vol. vii. pp. 215-217), 1826, and on Shelley in *The Censor*, 1829 (pp. 38-9, 49-51, 86), will not be excluded.

(The reproduction of Copyright Articles will of course depend on the consent of the copyright owners being obtained.   The Committee trust that the generosity usual in like cases will be extended to the Shelley Society.)

Series IV. will be a *Miscellaneous* one, and will include an edition of *The Cenci* for the Society's performances of the play ; *Shelley's Autobiography ;* a *Shelley Primer ;* a *Concordance to Shelley's Poetical Works*, a *Word- and Subject-Index to his Prose Works and Letters*, and such other works as may hereafter be decided on.

The Committee wish to get a large number of Branch Shelley Societies and Local Shelley Reading Clubs started out of London, and in its suburbs. They will be glad to appoint as *Local Honorary Secretaries* in any district such persons as will undertake to do what they can to promote the study of Shelley in their different localities.

The Committee also desire that all the effort and cost of getting up the performance of *The Cenci* in May next should not result in only one representation of this the greatest tragedy of modern drama.   They have therefore opened a Subscription to secure at least one repetition of the performance, and they have received promises to the amount of Fifteen Guineas.   Twice this sum would make the repetition certain ; and the Committee accordingly ask for further donations to the Fund.

The Committee are also prepared to receive Subscriptions for a performance of Shelley's *Hellas*, of which Dr. W. C. Sellé is setting the choruses to music.

PUBLICATIONS SUGGESTED.
Series I. *Papers.*

Part I. The Inaugural Address of the Rev. Stopford A. Brooke, M.A., and other Papers of the Session 1886, with Abstracts of the Discussions, Shelley " *Notes and Queries*," ' News,' &c.

Series II. *Facsimile Reprints of Shelley's Original Editions.*

1. *Adonais.* 4to. Pisa, 1821.[1] Edited by THOMAS J. WISE.
[*Now ready.*

2. Shelley's Review of Hogg's *Memoirs of Prince Alexy Haimatoff* in the *Critical Review* for December 1814 (not in facsimile), with Prof. Dowden's Article on it. Edited by THOMAS J. WISE. [*Now ready.*

3. *Alastor.* 1816. [*Now ready.*

4. *An Address to the Irish People.* 8vo. 1812. (*At press. Presented by* Mr. WALTER B. SLATER.)

5. *Epipsychidion.* 8vo. 1821.

6. *A Refutation of Deism.* 8vo. 1814.

7. *Œdipus Tyrannus.* 8vo. 1820.

8. *A Proposal for putting Reform to the Vote.* 8vo. 1817.

9. *The Necessity of Atheism.* 8vo. (Not dated, but 1811.) (*To be presented by* Mr. THOMAS J. WISE.)

10. *Proposals for an Association of Philanthropists.* 8vo. (Not dated, but 1812.)

11. *Posthumous Fragments of Margaret Nicholson.* 4to. 1810.[3]

12. *A Vindication of Natural Diet.* 12mo. 1813.[4]

13. *A Letter to Lord Ellenborough.* 8vo. (Not dated, but 1812.[5])

14. *Hellas, a Lyrical Drama.* 1822.

Series III. *Magazine Articles.*
SECTION 1.—*Biographical.*

(Many of the most important contributions to Shelley Biography are to be found in Periodical Literature. The following are those chiefly needed to fill up the gaps in the story of the Poet's life, and to correct the many inaccuracies of Hogg, Medwin, and other of his earlier biographers.)

PART I.—Statements by writers personally acquainted with Shelley.

1. "Percy Bysshe Shelley," in *Stockdale's Budget*, 1826-7. [*At press.*

2. Hogg's "Shelley at Oxford,"[6] in *The New Monthly Magazine*, January, February, April, July, October, and December, 1832, pp. 90-96, 136-144, 343-352, 65-73, 321-330, 505-513. [*At press.*

3. Hogg's "The History of Percy Bysshe Shelley's Expulsion from Oxford," in *The New Monthly Magazine*, for May, 1833, pp. 17-29. [*At press.*

4. "A Newspaper Editor's Reminiscences," in *Fraser*, No. cxxviii., June, 1841, pp. 699-710.

5. Peacock's "Memoirs of Shelley," in *Fraser*, No. cccxlii., June, 1858, pp. 643-659 ; No. ccclxi., January, 1860, pp. 92-109 ; No. ccclxiii., March, 1860, pp. 301-319 ; No. ccclxv., May, 1860, p. 738 ; and No. ccclxxxvii., March, 1862, pp. 343-346.

6. "Shelley, by One who Knew Him," by Thornton Hunt, in *The Atlantic Monthly*, February, 1863, pp. 184-204.

[1] For this, as much as £60 has been paid.
[2] From "Some Early Writings of Shelley," in *The Contemporary Review*, September, 1884.
[3] A "cut" copy of this in poor condition brought £53 in the Gardyne sale a few months since.
[4] A reprint of this tract has been published by the Vegetarian Society, Manchester.
[5] A penny reprint of this letter can be had of the Progressive Publishing Company, 28, Stonecutter Street, London, E.C.
[6] The six articles under this title ("Shelley at Oxford"), and the supplementary article recounting the Expulsion of Shelley and himself from Oxford, contributed by Hogg to *The New Monthly Magazine* in 1832 and 1833, form perhaps the most valuable portion of the two volumes which Hogg afterwards issued in 1858.

Part II.—Statements by later writers.

1. "Notes on Shelley's Birthplace," by W. Hale White, in *Macmillan's Magazine*, No. 233, vol. xxxix. pp. 461-465.

2 "On the Drowning of Shelley," by R. H. Horne, in *Fraser*, Nov. 1870, pp. 618-625.

3. "Shelley in 1812—13: An Unpublished Poem," by W. M. Rossetti, in *The Fortnightly Review*, January, 1871, pp. 67-85.

4. "Shelley's Last Days," by Dr. Garnett, in *The Fortnightly Review*, June 1, 1878, pp. 850-866.

5. "Improvisatore Sgricci in Relation to Shelley," by H.Buxton Forman, in *The Gentleman's Magazine*, January, 1880, pp. 115-123.

6. "Shelley's Life near Spezzia, his Death and Burials," by H. Buxton Forman, in *Macmillan's Magazine*, No. 247, May, 1880, pp. 43-58.

7. "Shelley and Mary," in *The Edinburgh Review*, No. 320, October, 1882, pp. 472-507.

Series III. Section 2.—*Contemporary Criticisms* of Shelley and his Works.

1. Review of "Zastrozzi" in *The Critical Review*, November, 1810, vol. xxi. 3rd series, 1811.

2. „ "St. Irvyne" in *The British Critic*, January, 1811.

3. „ "Poems by Victor and Cazire" in *The Poetical Register*, vol. viii., 1810-11, p. 617.

4. „ "Poems by Victor and Cazire" in *The British Critic*, April, 1811, vol. xxxvii. p. 408.

5. „ "Queen Mab" in *The Theological Inquirer*, 1815.

6. „ Poems in *The Mirror*, 1819.

7. „ "Alastor" in *Blackwood's Magazine*, November, 1819.

8. „ "Laon and Cythna," "The Revolt of Islam" in *The Quarterly*, No. xlii., September, 1819, pp. 460-471 (and "Rosalind and Helen," p. 470).

9. „ "Rosalind and Helen," and "Alastor" in *Blackwood's Magazine*, June and Nov., 1819; and "Adonais," in Dec., 1821.

10. „ "The Cenci" in *The Literary Gazette*, No. 167, April 1, 1820, pp. 209-210.

11. „ "Prometheus Unbound" in *The Literary Gazette*, No. 190, September 9, 1820, pp. 580-582.

12. „ "The Cenci" in *The New Monthly Magazine*, May, 1820.

13. „ "The Cenci" in *The London Magazine*, No. 5, May, 1820.

14. "*The Honeycomb*," No. 9. Saturday, August 12, 1820. "Portraits of the Metropolitan Poets." No. iii. Mr. Percy Bysshe Shelley, pp. 65-71

15. Review of "Queen Mab" in *The Literary Gazette*, No. 226, May 19, 1821, pp. 305-308.

16. „ "Epipsychidion," in *The Gossip*, June, 1821.

17. „ "Adonais" in *The Literary Gazette*, December 8, 1821, pp. 772-773.

18. „ "Prometheus Unbound" in *The Quarterly*, No. xli., December, 1821, pp. 168-180.

19. Leigh Hunt's 'Reviews' in *The Examiner*.

Series III. SECTION 3.

The most important *critical* articles—not necessarily excluding *reviews*—which have been contributed to later periodicals.

1. "The Life and Poetry of Shelley," by David Masson, in *Macmillan's Magazine*, June, 1860, pp. 338-350.

2. "The Poems of Shelley," in *The North British Review*, No. cv., October, 1870, pp. 30-58.

3. "Shelley's Metaphysics," by A. Cordery, in the *Dark Blue*, June, 1872, pp. 478-488.

4. "Shelley's 'Prometheus Unbound,'" by Arthur Clive, in *The Gentleman's Magazine*, No. lxxi., April, 1874, pp. 421-437.

5. Mr. W. M. Rossetti's two Lectures on Shelley, in the *Dublin University Magazine*, February and March, 1878, pp. 138-155, 262-277.

6. "Some Thoughts on Shelley," by Stopford A. Brooke, in *Macmillan's Magazine*, No. 248, June, 1880, pp. 124-135.

7. "The Prometheus of Æschylus and of Shelley," by the Rev. W. A. O'Conor, B.A., in *The Manchester Quarterly*, No. i., January, 1882, pp. 29-45.

8. "Shelley as a Teacher," by H. S. Salt, in *Temple Bar*, No. 264, November, 1882, pp. 365-377.

9. "A Note on Shelley," by James Thomson (B.V.) in *Progress*, vol. iii., No. 2, February, 1884, pp. 113-117.

10. "Some Early Writings of Shelley," by Professor Dowden, in *The Contemporary Review*, September, 1884, pp. 383-396.

Series IV. *Miscellaneous.*

1. "A Shelley Bibliography." Part I. Edited by H. Buxton Forman. [*Now ready*]. (Of this work, published by Reeves and Turner, the Shelley Society will issue a copy to each of its Members.)

2. "The Cenci" : a cheap edition for the Society's performance of the Tragedy in May, 1886, with an Introduction by H. Buxton Forman, and Notes by Alfred Forman.

3. "A Shelley Primer." (Messrs. Reeves and Turner, 196, Strand, W.C., will publish this, probably in 1886, and the Society will take a copy for each of its Members.)

4. Extracts from books relating to Shelley, compiled under the superintendence of H. Buxton Forman.

5. "Shelley's Autobiography." A collection of all passages by Shelley relating to himself and his works, with annotations by Wm. Michael Rossetti.

6. "A Concordance to Shelley's *Poetical Works*," and "a *General* and *Subject* Index to his *Prose Works* and *Letters*." Mrs. H. Buxton Forman has kindly placed her material for the former portion of this work at the Society's disposal. Mr. F. S. Ellis has been good enough to undertake *the editorship* of it. The Committee ask for volunteer help in both portions. Specimens will be ready soon. Offers of help for the *Concordance* are to be sent to Mr. F. S. Ellis, The Red House, Chelston, Torquay, and for the *Index* to H. B. Forman, 46, Marlborough Hill, St. John's Wood, London, N.W.

MEMBERS.

Abbott, T. C., Eastlegh, Queen's Road, Bowdon.
Armour, George A., 116, Home Insurance Buildings, Chicago, U.S.A.
Ashbee, C. R. A., King's College, Cambridge.
Axon, Wm. E. A., 66, Murray Street, Higher Broughton, Manchester.
Baddeley, St. Clair, 5, Albert Hall Mansions, Kensington Gore S.W
Bangs, Lemuel W., 188, Fleet Street, London, E.C.
Barnard, Mrs. Jas. Mason, Milton Hill, Milton, Mass., U.S.A.
Beaumont, Hubert, 144, Piccadilly, London, W.
Bell, Rev. Canon, D.D., Cheltenham.
Bell, Matthew, Temple Works, Cursitor Street, London, E.C.
Bennett, W. P.. 3, Bull Street, Birmingham.
Berdoe, E., Tynemouth House, Victoria Park Gate, London, E.
Best, John Vincent, 42, Lansdowne Gardens, South Lambeth, S.W.
Blind, Miss Mathilde, 10, Pembroke Square, Kensington, W.
Bradley, Miss Emily T., Deanery, Westminster.
Britton, John James, Heath House, Alcester, Warwickshire.
Brooke, Rev. Stopford A., 1, Manchester Square, London, W.
Burgin, Geo. B., 7, Dryden Road, Bush Hill Park, Enfield, N.
Call, Major, R.E., 26, Cheyne Walk, Chelsea, S.W.
Call, Mrs. C. F., 26, Cheyne Walk, Chelsea, S.W.
Call, W. M. W., 9, Addison Gardens, Kensington, W.
Call, Mrs. W., 9, Addison Gardens, Kensington, W.
Clough, William, 55, High Street, Chorlton-upon-Medlock.
Coles, C. B. Cowper, 95, Wigmore Street, London, W.
Craig, W. J., 8, Grenville Street, Brunswick Square, W.C.
Cyriax, Jules, 33, Douglas Road, Canonbury, London, N.
Dale, Andrew, 12, The Terrace, Camberwell Park, London, S.E.
Dallas-Glyn, Mrs., 13, Mount Street, Grosvenor Square, London, W.
Dobell, Bertram, 66, Queen's Crescent, Haverstock Hill, N.W.
Dowdeswell, Chas., Brantwood, Macaulay Road, Clapham Common, S.W.
Draper, E. Herbert, 42, Upper Bedford Place, London, W.C.
Dyer, Louis, Cambridge, Mass., U.S.A.
Ellis, F. S., The Red House, Chelston, Torquay.
Emrys-Jones, Dr. A., M.D., Oak Hill, Fallowfield, Manchester.
Firth, E. Harding, Leigh Side, Leigh Woods, Clifton, Bristol.
Forman, Alfred, 7, Holbeck Road, Stockwell, London, S.W.
Forman, George, 1, Upper Phillimore Place, Kensington, W.
Forman, H. Buxton, 46, Marlborough Hill, St. John's Wood, N.W.
Forman, Mrs., 5, Wilton Terrace, Camberwell Grove, S.E.
Fountain, Alfred, Highfield, Hillingdon, Uxbridge, Middlesex.
Frederickson, Charles W., 741, Lexington Avenue, New York City, U.S.A.
Frederickson, Mrs. Charles W., 741, Lexington Avenue, New York City,
    U.S.A.

Frost, H. F., 6, Southampton Street, Strand, London, W.C.
Furnivall, Dr. F. J., 3, St. George's Sq., Primrose Hill, N.W. (*Treasurer.*)
Galway, John, care of H. S. Sotheran & Co., 136, Strand, W.C.
Gaynor, Col. G. (104th Fusiliers), Junior United Service Club, London, S.W.
Grove, Miss Millicent S., Sir G. Grove's, Lower Sydenham, S.E.
Guildhall Library, E.C. (The Library Committee of the Corporation of
    the City of London. W. H. Overall, Librarian.)
Hall, C. G., Union Club, Trafalgar Square, London, W.
Hanson, E., 4, Chandos Street, Strand, London, W.C.
Harrison, Rev. W. A., St. Ann's Vicarage, S. Lambeth, S.W.
Hart, Horace, Controller, University Press, Oxford.
Hatchard, Mrs. H. Gibbons, Sylvanus Villa, 211, Maida Vale, W
Hatchard, Miss Marion L., Sylvanus Villa, 211, Maida Vale, W.
Holyoake, Percy, Fairbourne, King's Road, Clapham Park, S.W.
Home, F. Wyville, 1, Gordon Villas, Woodside, London, S.E.
Hueffer, Mrs., 72, Elsham Road, Addison Road, Kensington, W.
Hutt, Charles, 30, Hargrave Park Road, Junction Road, London, N.
Jacob, H. P. (of Bombay), Elm Grove, Dawlish.
Jones, Hy. A., The Hill House, Chalfont St. Peter, Slough, Bucks.
Kendal, Mrs., 145, Harley Street, London, W.
Kerr, Mrs. William, Glan William, Tan-y-Bwlch, Merioneth.
Lee, A. Collingwood, 2, Western Road, Ealing, W.
Lewis, W. B., African Steamship Company, 31, James Street, Liverpool.
Low, Miss Marie A., 50, Tavistock Square, London, W.C.
Macallister, Miss, Alcester, Warwickshire.
Milner, George, President of the Literary Club, Manchester.
Mosely, B. L., 55, Tavistock Square, London, W.C.
Mugliston, Rev. John, Newick House, Cheltenham.
Muir, Wm., 9, Angel Place, Edmonton, London, N.
Napier, Prof. A. S., Headington Hill, Oxford.
Neate, Mrs., 53, Belsize Park, London, N.W.
Palmer, W. J., 11, Pemberton Gardens, Upper Holloway, N.
Parkes, W. Kineton, Summerfield Crescent, Edgbaston.
Payne, John, 5, Lansdowne Place, Brunswick Square, W.C.
Perkins, Rev. Thos., Grammar School, Shaftesbury, Dorset.
Pierce, Prof. Jas. Mills, 4. Kirkland Place, Cambridge, Mass., U.S.A.
Posnett, Prof. H. Macaulay, Auckland University, New Zealand.
Potts, R. A., 26, South Audley Street, London, W.
Power, P. le Poer, Winter's Buildings, 32, St. Ann's Street, Manchester.
Preston, Sydney E., 88, Eaton Place, London, S.W. (*Honorary Secretary.*)
Rees, J. Rogers, Brecon Old Bank House, Cardiff.
Reeves, W., 196, Strand, London, W.C.
Reinagle, Mrs., 15, Twyford Place, Tiverton, N. Devon.
Revell, Wm. F., 58, Oxford Gardens, Notting Hill, London, W.
Richmond, John, Silverbank Villa, Cambuslang, Glasgow.

Roe, Bassett, 25, Richmond Road, Thornhill Crescent, N.
Rossetti, Wm. M., 5, Endsleigh Gardens, Euston Road, N.W. (*Chairman.*)
Rossiter, J. J., 12, Abbot's Walk, Forbury Gardens, Reading.
Samelson, A., M.D., 15, John Street, Manchester.
Sampson, Gerald N., Exeter College, Oxford.
Sarrazin, Gabriel, 21, Rue Vauquelin, Paris.
Schlengemann, E., 8, Wilberforce Road, Finsbury Park, London, N.
Scoffern, Mrs. Alice, 107, Clapham Road, S.W.
Scott, William Bell, 92, Cheyne Walk, Chelsea, S.W.
Sebley, F. J., 7, Pulling Terrace, Cambridge.
Sellon, Miss, The Hall, Sydenham, London, S.E.
Sheldon, Edw. W., University Club, Madison Square, New York, U.S.A.
Shelley, Sir Percy F., Bart., Boscombe Manor, Bournemouth, Hants.
Shelley, Lady, Boscombe Manor, Bournemouth, Hants.
Shorter, Clement K., 603, Holloway Road, London, N.
Silsbee, Edward, 65, Charles Street, Boston, Mass., U.S.A.
Simpson, Mrs., 1. Hargwyne Street, Stockwell, S.W.
Skipwith, Grey Hubert (Trinity Coll.), 26, Holywell Street, Oxford.
Slark, John, 12, Busby Place, Camden Road, London, N.W.
Slater, Walter B., 249, Camden Road, London, N.
Smithson, Mrs. Edward W., 13, Lendal, York.
Stephens, Arthur, 64, Cavendish Road, Brondesbury, London, N.W.
Stevenson, A. L., St. Andrewes, Clevedon.
Stock, Elliot, Fern Lodge, Millfield Lane, Highgate Rise, N.
Sweet, Hy., Mansfield Cottage, Heath Street, Hampstead, N.W.
Tegetmeier, W. B., Alexandra Grove, Finchley, London, N.
Tempest, Adolphus Vane, 112, Bond Street, London, W.
Thwaites, E. W., 16, Dunham Villas, Kensington, London, W.
Tozer, Rev. Henry Fanshawe, 10, Norham Gardens, Oxford.
Todhunter, Dr. J., Orchardcroft, Bedford Park, London, W.
Tyrer, C. E., Manchester and Salford Bank, Manchester.
Verrall, A. W., 3, Newnham Terrace, Cambridge.
Walhouse, M. J., 9, Randolph Crescent, Maida Vale, London, W.
Whiteley, George, 40, Liverpool Street, London, W.C.
Wilkinson, T. R., Manchester and Salford Bank, Manchester.
Wilmot, J. G., Junior Carlton Club, Pall Mall, London, S.W.
Wise, T. J., 127, Devonshire Road, Holloway, London, N.
Woods, Mrs. H. G., 28, Holywell, Oxford.   (124 *Members.*)

The Committee appeal to every Member to use his best efforts to increase the Society's numbers. Personal canvassing of all likely well-wishers is what is needed.

OTHER SOCIETIES.

New Shakspere, founded by Dr. Furnivall in 1873, to promote the in-
telligent study of SHAKSPERE, and to print his Works in their original
Spelling, with illustrative Treatises.   *President*, ROBERT BROWNING.
Director, F. J. FURNIVALL.   *Hon. Sec.*, K. Grahame, 65, Chelsea Gardens,
Chelsea Bridge Road, London, S.W.   Subscription One Guinea a year.

Chaucer, founded by Dr. Furnivall in 1868, to print all the best Chaucer
MSS., &c.   *Editor in chief*, F. J. Furnivall.   *Hon. Sec.*, W. A. Dalziel,
67, Victoria Road, Finsbury Park, N.   Subscription Two Guineas a year.

Wyclif, founded by Dr. Furnivall in 1882, to print Wyclif's Latin Works.
Editors, F. D. Matthew, Reginald Lane Poole, Dr. Rudolf Buddensieg,
Prof. Loserth, &c.   *Hon. Sec.*, J. W. Standerwick, General Post Office, E.C.
Subscription, One Guinea a year.

Early English Text, founded by Dr. Furnivall in 1864, to print all Early
English literary MSS.   *Director*, F. J. Furnivall.   *Hon. Sec.* W. A. Dalziel,
67, Victoria Road, Finsbury Park, N.   One Guinea a year for the *Original
Series* of prints of MSS. only, and One Guinea for the *Extra Series* of
prints from MSS. or black-letters of Texts before printed.

Ballad, founded by Dr. Furnivall in 1868, to print all early English MS.
Ballads, and reprint the Roxburghe, Bagford and other collections of
printed Ballads.   *Editor in chief*, The Rev. J. W. Ebsworth, M.A.
Hon. Sec., W. A. Dalziel, 67, Victoria Rd., London, N.   £1 1s. a year.

Browning, founded in July 1881, by Dr. Furnivall and Miss E. H. Hickey,
to further the study of ROBERT BROWNING's poems, and to print papers on
them and Illustrations of them.   Subscription, One Guinea a year.
Hon. Sec., J. Dykes Campbell, 29, Albert Hall Mansions, Kensington
Gore, London, S.W.

Philological, founded in 1842, to investigate the Structure, Affinities, and
the History of Languages.   *Hon. Sec.*, F. J. Furnivall.   One Guinea
entrance, and one a year.   Parts I. and II. of the Society's English
Dictionary, for which material has been collecting for 28 years, have
been lately issued, edited by Dr. J. A. H. Murray, and publisht by the
Clarendon Press, Oxford.

Wagner, to promote the study of his Musical and other works, and the
performance of his Operas at Bayreuth.   *Hon. Sec.* for England, B. L.
Mosely, 55, Tavistock Square, London, W.C.   Subscription, Ten Shillings
a year.

Shakspere Quarto Facsimiles, 10s. 6d. each, or 6s. if the whole series is
taken, edited by F. J. Furnivall, Prof. Dowden, Mr. P. A. Daniel, Mr.
H. A. Evans, Mr. Arthur Symons, Mr. T. Tyler, and other Shakspere
scholars.   B. Quaritch, 15, Piccadilly, London, W.   (Twenty Facsimiles
have been published, and ten more will be ready soon.   The Series will
be completed in 1886.)